Copyright © 2024 by Annette Bridges

www.annettebridges.com

Published by Ranch House Press

All rights reserved. Except as permitted under the U.S. Copyright Act of 1976, no part of this publication may be reproduced, distributed, or transmitted in any form or by any means, or stored in a database or retrieval system, without the prior written permision of the author.

The coffee messages in this book don't belong to any one author. All have unknown authors edited by Annette for this book. It could undoubtedly be said that the "cattitudes" in this book have been exclaimed, felt and believed by any and all coffee lovers at some point in their collective lives.

Original photographs of Snowbaby were taken by Annette Bridges.

Designed and Illustrated by Janie Owen-Bugh
www.janieowenbugh.com

Printed in the United States of America.

ISBN 978-1-946371-49-2

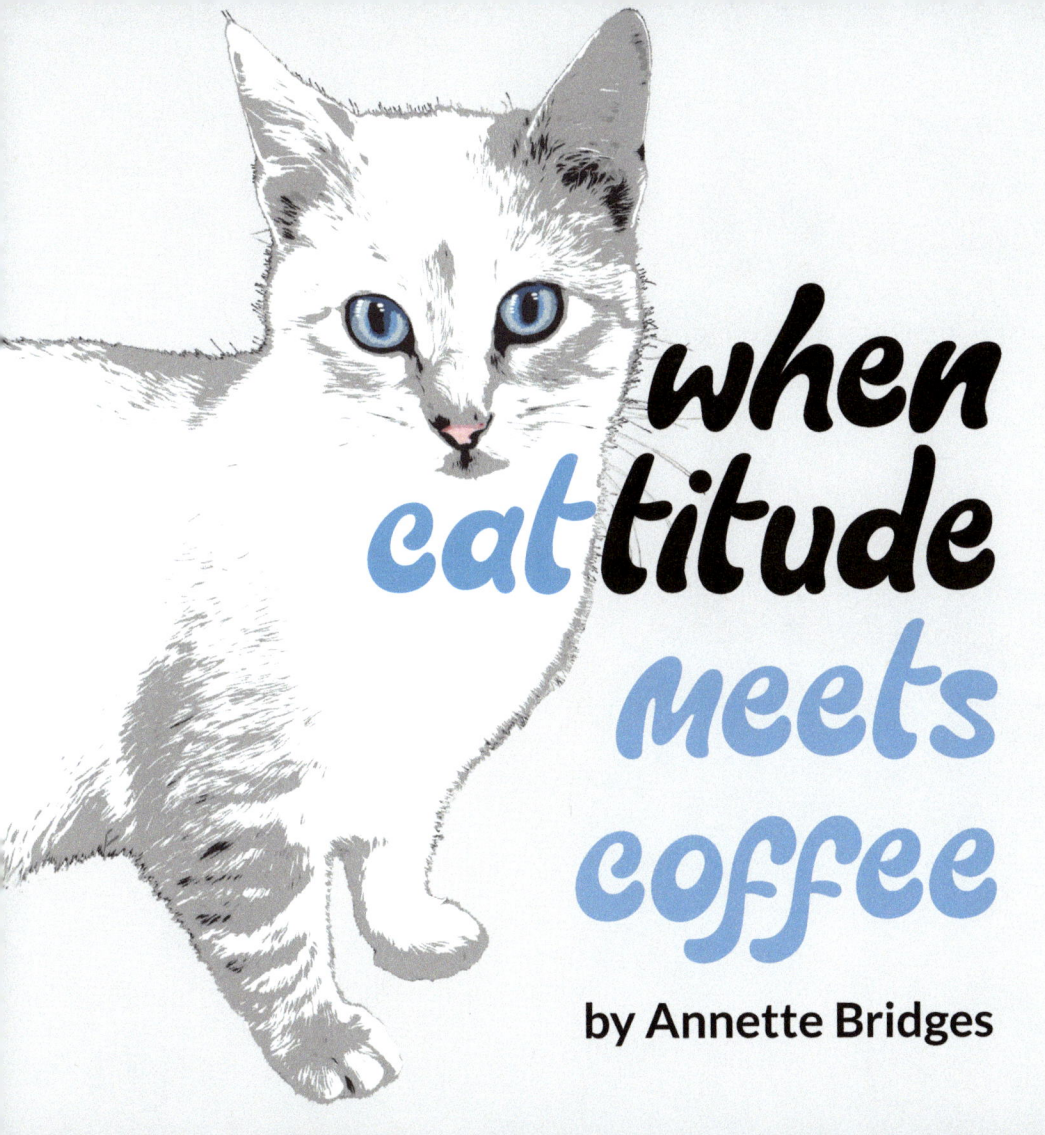

when cattitude meets coffee

by Annette Bridges

DON'T **UNDERESTIMATE YOURSELF.**

You can do hard things.

Like **making coffee** in the morning **before** you've **had** any **coffee.**

Love is in the **AIR** and it smells like **COFFEE**

May your coffee kick in before reality does.

Life without coffee is like *something* without *something.*

Sorry, I haven't had any *coffee, yet.*

To make me HAPPY, make me COFFEE, bring me COFFEE, be COFFEE

Sometimes you can go hours without drinking **COFFEE.**

It's called **SLEEPING.**

STRESSED, BLESSED, AND COFFEE OBSESSED.

Everyone *should* believe *in* something.

Coffee? Yes, Please.

I believe I will have another coffee.

Last night I wanted to drink COFFEE.

This morning I'm drinking COFFEE.

Follow your dreams, PEOPLE!

NEVER trust ANYONE who DOESN'T drink COFFEE.

About the author and her cat

Annette Bridges and her husband have been Texas cattle ranchers for over forty years. She writes a monthly column for North Texas Farm & Ranch magazine titled, *"When a city girl goes country."*

Annette loves to write, doodle, paint and take photos of her furry friends. She uses her art and photography to create all kinds of products. *When Cattitude Meets Coffee* is her latest creation.

The beautiful white feline with gorgeous blue eyes featured in this book was once a feral kitten Annette named Snowbaby. She lives in the tree where she was born in Annette's backyard. Folks see her catio that surrounds her tree and think she's one lucky kitty.

Their barn mamma cat had her kittens in the hollow of the old mulberry tree in their backyard. For some reason when Snowbaby's mamma moved her kittens to the barn, she deserted poor little Snowbaby.

Naturally, they started providing food and water to the tiny white, blue-eyed feline beauty. Annette's husband built a platform in her tree where they placed an insulated, waterproof house.

Sadly, an intense summer storm caused her tree to split in half. When they rushed outside in the rain to check on Snowbaby, she was sitting on a broken limb soaking wet. She would not leave her beloved tree.

Since it was very clear that Snowbaby did not want to live in the barn with their other farm cats, Annette's husband managed to save her tree trunk and parts of some limbs. He built a new platform with a roof for her treehouse. A catio was also built that fully enclosed her tree to provide the

security she needed. There are many enemies to kittens when you live in the country including other feral cats, coyotes and owls.

Snowbaby loves living in her catio. She eventually got brave enough to let her feet touch the ground of her catio, too. She's a happy kitty! And she even lets her human mamma hold her now. Annette always says she isn't sure if she adopted Snowbaby or if Snowbaby adopted her.

Annette lived half of her life before trying coffee. Mountain Dew was her go-to for caffeine. She didn't marry a coffee drinker so honestly drinking coffee was never something she thought about. Her world changed when they were celebrating a wedding anniversary on the veranda of a southern plantation house in Mississippi. The gracious hostess served their coffee in exquisite vintage porcelain cups. The aroma was magical and mesmerizing. She was immediately transported back to her grandmother's house as she recalled that fragrant, earthy, sweet smell that permeated throughout her house every morning. Annette's hubby added the perfect amount of cream and sugar to their cups. Soothing, satisfying and wonderfully balanced and refreshing describes her first sip. She was shocked at the yumminess and sad to think of all the years she missed having coffee in her life. She was hooked!

Coffee and Snowbaby are two of Annette's most unexpected loves so it seemed most-fitting to publish a book celebrating both.

You can learn more about Annette and read all of her magazine columns on her website at annettebridges.com

Catio life

other titles by Annette Bridges

BOOKS:

Mamma Said So
20 Pearls of Wisdom from a Southern Sage

101 Things Women Want from Their Men
Written collectively by hundreds of women who shared their advice.

A Dachshund Tale
Lessons learned from my dog.

Oh, How the Years Fly By!
A whimsical inspirational quote book.

The Gospel According to Mamma
One mother's philosophy on love, God, money, aging, decisions, change, and much more.

Be Queen of Your Life
A savvy mom helps daughters command and rule their lives.

Have Lipstick, Will Travel
How to reimagine your life, purpose, and hair color.

JOURNALS:

Okay, We Grew Old Together… Now What?
A couple's journal.

My Furry Friend
A keepsake journal.

Jot Journals
18 themed pocket-sized journals.

Color Your World Journal Series
18 themed large journals.

COLORING BOOKS:

Color-N-Doodle Your World
An inspiring collection of coloring pages with your own space to doodle and create.

Oh, How the Years Fly By!
A whimsical adult coloring book.

BOOKS FOR CHILDREN:

Lady and Bella: Totally Different, Totally Friends
A coloring storybook for children.

Lady and Bella: Totally Friends Journal
Especially for children.

Lady and Bella's Alphabet Kitchen
A to Z recipes for kid cooks.

www.ingramcontent.com/pod-product-compliance
Lightning Source LLC
Chambersburg PA
CBHW041725070526
44586CB00001B/4